W9-BHK-052

# Jo MacDonald

## Had a Garden

By Mary Quattlebaum        Illustrated by Laura J. Bryant

Dawn Publications

*To Christy, with love* — MQ
*To Paula* — LJB

Copyright © 2012 Mary Quattlebaum
Illustrations copyright © 2012 Laura J. Bryant

Library of Congress Cataloging-in-Publication Data
Quattlebaum, Mary.
  Jo MacDonald had a garden / by Mary Quattlebaum ; illustrated by Laura J. Bryant. -- 1st ed.
      p. cm.
  Summary: In this version of the classic song "Old MacDonald Had a Farm," the farmer's granddaughter plants a garden which provides a place for birds, insects, and other wild creatures to shelter and nest. Backmatter presents facts and activities related to this lively ecosystem.
  Includes bibliographical references.
  ISBN 978-1-58469-164-8 (hardback) -- ISBN 978-1-58469-165-5 (pbk.)
1.  Folk songs, English--United States--Texts. [1. Gardening--Songs and music. 2. Garden ecology--Songs and music. 3. Garden animals--Songs and music. 4. Folk songs--United States.]  I. Bryant, Laura J., ill. II. Title.
  PZ8.3.Q25Jl 2012
  782.42--dc23
  [E]

                          2011037920


Book design and production by Patty Arnold, *Menagerie Design & Publishing*

Manufactured by Regent Publishing Services, Hong Kong,
Printed December, 2011, in ShenZhen, Guangdong, China

10 9 8 7 6 5 4 3 2 1
First Edition

**Dawn Publications**
12402 Bitney Springs Road
Nevada City, CA 95959
530-274-7775
nature@dawnpub.com

Jo MacDonald had a garden,
    E – I – E – I – O.
And in that garden was some sun,
    E – I – E – I – O.
      With a glow-glow here
        And a glow-glow there,
    Here a glow, there a glow,
      Everywhere a glow-glow.
    Jo MacDonald had a garden,
      E – I – E – I – O.

And in that garden was some soil,
E – I – E – I – O.
With a dig-dig here
And a dig-dig there,
Here a dig, there a dig,
Everywhere a dig-dig.
Jo MacDonald had a garden,
E – I – E – I – O.

And in that garden was a worm,
E – I – E – I – O.
   With a wiggle-wiggle here
      And a wiggle-wiggle there,
Here a wiggle, there a wiggle,
   Everywhere a wiggle-wiggle.
Jo MacDonald had a garden.
   E – I – E – I – O.

And in that garden she planted seeds,
E – I – E – I – O.
With a pat-pat here
And a pat-pat there,
Here a pat, there a pat,
Everywhere a pat-pat.
Jo MacDonald had a garden,
E – I – E – I – O.

And in that garden she had some water,
E – I – E – I – O.
With a sprinkle-sprinkle here
And a sprinkle-sprinkle there,
Here a sprinkle, there a sprinkle,
Everywhere a sprinkle-sprinkle.
Jo MacDonald had a garden,
E – I – E – I – O.

And in that garden flew a bird,
E – I – E – I – O.
With a flit-flit here
And a flit-flit there,
Here a flit, there a flit,
Everywhere a flit-flit.
Jo MacDonald had a garden,
E – I – E – I – O.

And in that garden sprouted plants,
E – I – E – I – O.
With a grow-grow here
And a grow-grow there,
Here a grow, there a grow,
Everywhere a grow – grow.

Jo MacDonald had a garden,
Grow and GROW and

OH!

Radish

And in that garden she had some food,
E – I – E – I – O.
    With a pick-pick here
        And a pick-pick there,
Here a pick, there a pick,
        Everywhere a pick-pick.
Jo MacDonald had a garden,
    E – I – E – I – O.

And in that garden she made a treat,
E – I – E – I – O.
With a yum-yum here
And a yum-yum there,
Here a yum, there a yum,
Everywhere a yum-yum.
Jo MacDonald had a garden,
E – I – E – I – O.

And then that garden had a rest,
E – I – E – I – O.
With a shh-shh here
And a shh-shh there,
Here a shh, there a shh,
Everywhere a shh-shh.
Jo MacDonald had a garden,
E – I – E – I – O.

And to that garden came the spring,
E – I – E – I – O.
With a glow-glow here
And a dig-dig there,
With a wiggle-wiggle here
And a pat-pat there,

With a sprinkle-sprinkle here
And a flit-flit there,
With a grow-grow here
And a pick-pick there.

Here a yum.
There a yum.
Everywhere a yum-yum.

Jo MacDonald had a garden,

E – I – E – HELLO!

All the wild visitors have returned!
Can you find all seven creatures? All seven plants?
Turn the page for their names. Now, go back to the
beginning and find when each one arrives.

## A New Twist on an Old Song

The song "Old MacDonald Had a Farm" has taught generations of children about farm animals. Now the farmer's granddaughter, Jo MacDonald, and her cousin, Mike, use the traditional tune to introduce a garden community. Children can follow along with Jo, making the sounds, mimicking her movements, and creating their own "pretend" garden as the story progresses.

## The Garden Community

A garden is part of the greater community of plants and animals. Like Jo, you can grow your garden in a way that helps both people and wild creatures. This is important because wildlife loses food and shelter when we build houses, stores, and roads upon its *habitat*—the place where it naturally lives. Wild creatures benefit from gardens, and gardens benefit from them, too.

Choose your garden spot carefully. You need sun, rich dirt (often called *soil*), and water for healthy plants. Jo planted four kinds of seeds and Mike planted two kinds of seedlings. Each plant has six parts: *roots, stem, leaves, flowers, fruit,* and *seeds*. Some parts are edible. In fact, kids are more than twice as likely to eat fruits and vegetables if they grow them. The following seven creatures and seven plants appear in Jo's garden, starting with the page that begins the song.

**Blackhaw viburnums** are *native* plants, found naturally in a particular habitat. Native plants provide shelter, nesting places, and food (nectar, berries, leaves, and nuts) for wildlife. Jo put her garden near the viburnum so her wild visitors would have a place to shelter and nest. It was the only plant that did not die during the winter.

**Cardinals** are known by their head crests and plumage: red for males and brownish for females. Cardinals eat insects, seeds, and berries, and feed insects to their nestlings. Sunflower seeds can help them survive the winter since they do not migrate. The cardinal is the official state bird of Illinois, Indiana, Kentucky, North Carolina, Ohio, Virginia, and West Virginia.

**Painted lady butterflies** are found throughout the world. When flying from flower to flower for nectar, they pollinate the plants. In Jo's garden, the coneflower provides nectar and the sunflower is a host plant for its eggs and hungry caterpillars (larvae).

**Earthworms** are a gardener's best friend. They eat dead leaves, and their poop, called *casts*, helps to create rich soil. Earthworms hibernate deep in the soil in winter. Many animals eat earthworms, including robins and toads.

**Ladybugs** and their larvae feed on many types of insect pests, including aphids, mites, and mealybugs. These beetles have red shells with black spots.

**Tomato** plants produce a large red or yellow berry. Often called a vegetable because it's not sweet, the tomato is really a fruit because it contains seeds.

**Radish** plants have crunchy, edible roots, a popular salad vegetable.

**Lettuce** has edible leaves, a favorite salad vegetable.

**Summer Squash** plants, like tomatoes, produce large, non-sweet fruit commonly known as a vegetable.

**Coneflowers**, or echinacea, are native plants that provide nectar and seeds for wildlife.

**Bumblebees** gather nectar from flowers and, in turn, pollinate plants. These insects rarely sting unless they are bothered. People do not harvest honey from bumblebees but from a bee called a honey bee.

**Toads** eat garden pests such as slugs, snails, flies, and other insects. They breathe and drink through their skin. They like moist gardens with places to hide.

**Sunflowers** provide nectar for bees and butterflies, seeds for birds (and people), an egg-laying place for certain butterflies, and food for caterpillars.

**Robins** migrate south in winter but return to the north in early spring. These birds lay blue-green eggs and mostly eat earthworms.

## Indoor Activities

Enjoy year-round fun with Jo and Mike! You can find answers to these questions in the descriptions above. Check www.dawnpub.com for additional activities.

- With each new illustration, at least one new creature or plant enters the garden until the robins arrive — seven types of creatures and seven types of plants. Can you find and name them?

- What does the butterfly eat? The bumblebee? How do they help plants?

- Name the four vegetables planted by Jo and Mike. What part of these plants did Jo use in her garden treat? What was the treat?

- A vegetable is any edible part of a plant except for a sweet fruit or seed. Summer squash is really a fruit, although it's usually called a vegetable. So is another "vegetable" in Jo's garden. Which one?

- Jo's mystery seed grew into what kind of plant?

- Find the birds that stayed during the winter. What are they eating? Many plants die in the winter but some remain. Can you find the one plant in Jo's garden that lived through the winter?

- Draw a picture of the sunflower. Can you name its six parts?

- Draw a picture of your favorite garden creature. Can you draw what it eats or where it rests?

- Want to plant a seed like Jo and watch it grow? Add soil to a small plastic tub and plant a summer squash or sunflower seed. Put it in a sunny window. Keep the soil moist. A tiny stem and leaves should appear in 10 to 14 days. In a week or two, you should be able to plant the seedling outdoors and watch as it continues to grow, flower, and even produce fruit (in the case of the squash plant).

## How to Be a Gardener Like Jo

**Help the Wildlife in Your Garden:** Like Jo and Mike, you can plant **coneflowers** and **sunflowers** to provide nectar for bees and butterflies, seeds for birds, and egg-laying plants for butterflies. A **large, flat rock** offers a spot for butterflies to rest and warm their wings. A **birdbath** provides drinking and bathing water for birds, and a broken flower pot could become a **toad home**. As the weather grows colder, food becomes scarce. Like Jo, you can hang **bird feeders** and **scatter seeds** for birds that don't *migrate* (travel to warmer places) in the winter.

**Make Observations:** Record what you planted and the date. When did leaves and stems first appear? When did you harvest or pick what you grew? Did some plants grow better than others? What garden treats did you make and share? What fruit or vegetable did you or your friends like best? You can also write about, draw, and photograph wild visitors. What birds and insects visited each season? What did they do and what seemed to attract them? Which creatures stayed and which migrated during the winter? Keep your observations in one notebook or journal so you have a record of how a place changes over time. Share your observations with others.

## Help for Young Gardeners

The following resources will help you choose and cultivate the most suitable seeds and plants for your area, including native varieties: American Horticultural Society's Youth Gardens program, www.ahs.org/youth_gardening; Junior Master Gardener Program, www.jmgkids.us; Ladybird Johnson Wildflower Center, www.wildflower.org; National Gardening Association, www.kidsgardening.org; and National Wildlife Federation, www.nwf.org/garden.

**There's Much More:** For playful ways to help youngsters learn about plant parts and vegetables and to create crafts such as toad homes and indoor sweet potato-top gardens, get downloadable activities and recipes at www.dawnpub.com.

**Mary Quattlebaum** grew up in the country surrounded by woods and fields. She first learned about plants and wildlife by helping to tend her family's large vegetable garden and planting wildlife gardens as 4-H projects. Mary now lives in Washington, DC, where she and her family enjoy watching the birds, squirrels, butterflies, and other wild visitors to their backyard habitat. She is the author of many children's books and teaches in the Vermont College MFA program in Writing for Children and Young Adults. Mary loves visiting schools and talking with kids. See her website, www.maryquattlebaum.com.

**Laura Bryant** always enjoyed drawing and was fortunate to have a creative mother and enthusiastic art teachers in school. She attended the Maryland Institute College of Art in Baltimore where she studied painting, printmaking and sculpture. After many years of searching for her "ultimate job," she found it when in 1997 she started illustrating children's books. She has now illustrated over 20 books, including *If You Were My Baby* published by Dawn Publications. Laura says, "Illustrating children's books has given me an endless supply of creative freedom and joy." See her website, www.laurabryant.com.

## ALSO IN THIS SERIES BY MARY QUATTLEBAUM

*Jo MacDonald Saw a Pond* — Yes, old MacDonald had a pond, too! Jo sketches what she sees there and witnesses a wild surprise. E—I—E—I—O!

## A FEW OTHER NATURE AWARENESS BOOKS FROM DAWN PUBLICATIONS

*Molly's Organic Farm* is based on the true story of homeless cat that found herself in the wondrous world of an organic farm. Seen through Molly's eyes, the reader discovers the interplay of nature that grows wholesome food.

*In the Trees, Honey Bees* offers a inside-the-hive view of a wild colony, along with solid information about these remarkable and valuable creatures.

*The "Over" Series* — Kids sing, clap, and thinking these books are entertainment while adults think they are educational! Patterned on the classic old tune of "Over in the Meadow," this series by Marianne Berkes includes *Over in the Ocean, Over in the Jungle, Over in the Arctic, Over in the Forest,* and *Over in Australia.*

*The "Mini-Habitat" Series* — Beginning with the insects to be found under a rock (*Under One Rock: Bugs, Slugs and Other Ughs*) and moving on to other small habitats (around old logs, on flowers, cattails, cactuses, and in a tidepool), author Anthony Fredericks has a flair for introducing children to interesting "neighborhoods" of creatures. Field trips between covers!

**Dawn Publications** is dedicated to inspiring in children a deeper understanding and appreciation for all life on Earth. You can browse through our titles, download resources for teachers, and order at www.dawnpub.com or call 800-545-7475.